SOLVE

FINDING GOD'S SOLUTIONS
IN A WORLD OF PROBLEMS

SOLVE

FINDING GOD'S SOLUTIONS IN A WORLD OF PROBLEMS

TALBOT DAVIS

SOLVE

FINDING GOD'S SOLUTIONS IN A WORLD OF PROBLEMS

Copyright © 2016 by Abingdon Press

Scripture quotations unless noted otherwise are from the Common English Bible. Copyright © 2011 by the Common English Bible. All rights reserved. Used by permission. *www.CommonEnglishBible.com.*

Scripture quotations marked (NIV) are taken from the Holy Bible, New International Version®, NIV®. Copyright © 1973, 1978, 1984, 2011 by Biblica, Inc.™ Used by permission of Zondervan. All rights reserved worldwide. *www.zondervan.com.* The "NIV" and "New International Version" are trademarks registered in the United States Patent and Trademark Office by Biblica, Inc.™

Library of Congress Cataloging-in-Publication Data

CIP Data has been requested.

16 17 18 19 20 21 22 23 24 25—10 9 8 7 6 5 4 3 2 1

MANUFACTURED IN THE UNITED STATES OF AMERICA

CONTENTS

INTRODUCTION

Finding Solutions

A lot of people are good at pointing out problems.

In fact, some are expert at it. They have a knack for pointing out all that is wrong with people, situations, governments, and churches.

Especially churches.

Am I describing anyone you know?

Am I describing you?

If so—if you know someone or you are someone who has a real knack for pointing out problems—please know that this is no great skill. *Anyone* can do that. I'd even say that it's one of the lowest common denominators of the human race.

So while most people are adept at pointing out problems, there is another kind of person I am hoping to grow with this book.

I'm hoping to help you become one of the few, the proud, the brave who *pinpoint solutions*.

A few years ago, I heard about a company that developed an entire cadre of workers devoted to providing solutions to their customers' problems. They called this elite team ***Solutionists***.

So that's what I invite you to become as you read this book: a *solutionist*. I want to challenge you to abandon your expertise at pointing out problems and, instead, learn to excel at pinpointing solutions. It's what I desire for the people of Good Shepherd Church, where I serve as pastor, and for the audience reading *Solve.*

And together, you and I get to have a master teacher on the path to becoming solutionists: the Old Testament figure of Nehemiah.

Nehemiah is an overlooked yet vital figure in the Old Testament story. Here are some highlights you need to know about this first solutionist:

- Much of the book that bears his name is best understood in modern terms as a *memoir*—a style of writing that's quite rare in the biblical library. It is written primarily in the first person, it does not pretend to be an exhaustive biography of its author, and the facts are arranged in such a way to make the memoirist look good.
- Nehemiah's life and ministry takes place during one of the least understood epochs in biblical history: the post-exilic period—so named because during this time, the children of Judah return from their exile in Babylon, re-establish their homeland in the environs around Jerusalem, and discover to their dismay that life isn't much better after the exile than it was before.
- Nehemiah steps into the leadership void of the post-exilic community and empowers the people to rebuild their wall and reestablish their city. Modern parallels would include those who helped rebuild Europe after World War II and those who helped with New York City in the days following September 11, 2001.

• Chronologically, then, Nehemiah follows the major prophets of Jeremiah and Ezekiel and serves as a contemporary to some of the minor prophets, such as Haggai.

I mentioned earlier that Nehemiah is an "overlooked" figure. That's a great shame of so much Bible teaching; because if we somehow miss Nehemiah, we miss a figure of resolute action and unbridled optimism.

In the pages that follow, you will see how Nehemiah leveraged his bias toward action and bent toward optimism to mobilize and empower all of Jerusalem to take ownership of its future.

He moved them from observers to participants.

From victims to victors.

From people who see problems to people who solve them.

He created a city full of *solutionists*.

May Nehemiah inspire that same movement in the life of your family, your workplace, and your church!

Talbot Davis

1

PROBLEMISTS

Let your ear be attentive and your eyes open to hear the prayer of your servant. (Nehemiah 1:6a)

I remember exactly where I was when I first had the idea for the sermon series that formed the basis for this book. At Good Shepherd Church, we support a lot of recovery programs, which hold their meetings at our Zoar Road campus. Many of these meetings are open to the public so that you can attend them even if you are not a participant. I drop by these public meetings periodically just to show those communities how much Good Shepherd loves what they are about. Anyway, a while back I was in an open meeting of Alcoholics Anonymous, with probably forty people there. As usual, I was awestruck by the raw spirituality of the environment. During the sharing time, a man said the following words that still stick with me: "We don't have a drinking *problem*. We have a drinking *solution*. We've got all kinds of problems—marriage, parents, self-esteem, money—and what we all have in common in this room is that our solution to those problems has been to drink them away!" I heard that and immediately I thought, "I may have just heard the single most brilliant insight into anything, anywhere in my life." So I ran out to the car and wrote it down. Six months later I was preaching the first sermon in a series about our solutions and our problems.

That's why the first chapter in *Solve* is called "Problemists." As we jump from this insight from Alcoholics Anonymous into Scripture and back into our lives, it fascinates me how much we confuse our problems and our solutions. I think you'll see, as I have found, that our so-called solutions often end up being the sources of problems. And what's needed in those situations is for us to turn away from our false solutions to true ones.

This entire book, from faux solutions to real ones, comes from the best memoir in the biblical library, Nehemiah. You see, Scripture is full of many different genres of writing. The Bible contains poetry, lists, laws, narratives, letters, parables, and more. And much of the Book of Nehemiah can be understood as a memoir. Like modern memoirs, it's written in the first person, sort of selective with details; and as we are going to see, the facts are arranged in such a way as to put Nehemiah in a good light. This memoir gives us an account of Nehemiah's activity in rebuilding the wall of Jerusalem, as well as his role in building up the social and worship life of the people in the city.

To understand fully the events of Nehemiah, we have to delve back into history a little bit. As the book opens up, its main action—the circumstances that make up the dilemma to be solved—has already occurred. It's like a play in which the biggest action has taken place offstage, and the characters are dealing with the aftermath rather than the initial event itself.

Here's the deal: It's 445 B.C., during the reign of the Persian king Artaxerxes I. A century and a half earlier, in 587 B.C., the kingdom of Judah and the city of Jerusalem had been conquered by the Babylonian empire. Jerusalem and the Temple where the people worshipped the LORD were destroyed, and the best and brightest of its citizens were transported to Babylon to live in exile. This was a huge, devastating event for God's people. But then, some fifty years later, the Babylonian empire itself was conquered. The Persians defeated Babylon and eventually came to rule a vast empire covering that area of the world. In 539 B.C., the victorious Persian king Cyrus allowed the people of Judah to return home to Jerusalem to rebuild the Temple that had been destroyed.

Initial efforts to rebuild the Temple met with resistance and obstacles, and the new Temple wasn't completed until 516 B.C. And what's more, the city itself remained without walls, which had been broken down in the destruction of 587. Jerusalem was still, by and large, a city of ruins. The people who returned in 539 had come home to a bombed out, burned up city, and the reconstruction of the Temple was only the first step of many. Nearly a century later, there remained much to be done; and social problems such as unfair lending practices compounded their troubles. By the time Nehemiah opens, in 445 B.C., it's as if the people of Jerusalem have started an ambitious reclamation project, but it was very poorly done. The city very likely felt and looked like one of the sad Syrian places you see on TV today: burned up, hollowed out, devoid of both leadership and hopefulness.

That's the situation that forms the backdrop to the Book of Nehemiah. Those are the circumstances that Nehemiah responds to in Chapter 1. Through his reaction to hearing the news of Jerusalem's sad state, we can learn a lot about problems and solutions. Here is the opening of Nehemiah:

> [1] These are the words of Nehemiah, Hacaliah's son.
> In the month of Kislev, in the twentieth year, while I was in the fortress city of Susa, [2] Hanani, one of my brothers,

came with some other men from Judah. I asked them about the Jews who had escaped and survived the captivity, and about Jerusalem.

³ They told me, "Those in the province who survived the captivity are in great trouble and shame! The wall around Jerusalem is broken down, and its gates have been destroyed by fire!"

⁴ When I heard this news, I sat down and wept. I mourned for days, fasting and praying before the God of heaven. ⁵ I said:

"Lord God of heaven, great and awesome God, you are the one who keeps covenant and is truly faithful to those who love you and keep your commandments. ⁶ Let your ear be attentive and your eyes open to hear the prayer of your servant, which I now pray before you night and day for your servants, the people of Israel.

"I confess the sins of the people of Israel, which we have committed against you. Both I and my family have sinned. ⁷ We have wronged you greatly. We haven't kept the commandments, the statutes, and the ordinances that you commanded your servant Moses.

⁸ "Remember the word that you gave to your servant Moses when you said, 'If you are unfaithful, I will scatter you among the peoples. ⁹ But if you return to me and keep my commandments by really doing them, then, even though your outcasts live under distant skies, I will gather them from there and bring them to the place that I have chosen as a dwelling for my name.' ¹⁰ They are your servants

and your people. They are the ones whom you have redeemed by your great power and your strong hand.

[11] "LORD, let your ear be attentive to the prayer of your servant and to the prayer of your servants who delight in honoring your name. Please give success to your servant today and grant him favor in the presence of this man!"

At that time, I was a cupbearer to the king.

Now, the first thing to notice is that of all this—the sad state of Jerusalem, with its broken-down walls and burned-out gates—is *not* Nehemiah's particular problem. Look at the last part of verse 1: "while I was in the fortress city of Susa." Susa was an important city of the Persian empire, hundreds of miles away from Jerusalem, in modern-day Iran. The end of verse 11 gives more indication of Nehemiah's circumstances: "At that time, I was a cupbearer to the king." Nehemiah was serving in the court of the king of Persia; he was far, far away from his homeland. He had probably never lived there, anyway, since it had been nearly 150 years since his ancestors were deported from Jerusalem. When the Book of Nehemiah begins, the main character is right next to the seat of power, living in the lap of luxury. He doesn't need to bother with any of these problems about Jerusalem; he could carry on with his life perfectly well without concerning himself with such things.

But then Nehemiah receives a report from the front lines in verses 2-3. One of his brothers, Hanani, has recently been to Judah and has returned with some people who live there. When Nehemiah asks about the condition of the city and the people, they say, "Those in the province who survived the captivity are in great trouble and shame! The wall around Jerusalem is broken down,

ALL THIS IS NOT NEHEMIAH'S PROBLEM.

and its gates have been destroyed by fire!" (Nehemiah 1:3). Wall broken. Gates burned. People in great trouble and shame. Recent troubles sound an awful lot like past destruction. In 587 B.C., there was destruction and exile. In 539, the people returned. But almost a hundred years later, in 445 B.C., Jerusalem is still in shambles.

The question we have in reading his is, why? What got the people of God out from under the protection of God and into this kind of situation in the first place? Why are their very lives broken and burned?

Well, do you remember how I said that so much of the stage-setting action in Nehemiah occurs off stage? In this case, so much of the action occurs in the books of 1 and 2 Kings. The destruction of Jerusalem in 587 B.C. is not the whole story. Much of the books of 1 and 2 Kings lead up to this event, which is recorded in 2 Kings 25. The story these books tell is largely one of unfaithfulness, with Israel and Judah worshipping other gods besides the Lord. Nehemiah summarizes this story well as part of his prayer in Nehemiah 1:6-7: "I confess the sins of the people Israel, which we have committed against you. Both I and my family have sinned. We have wronged you greatly. We haven't kept the commandments, the statutes, and the ordinances that you commanded your servant Moses."

"We haven't kept the commandments." Do you remember the first of those commandments? "You must have no other gods before me" (Exodus 20:3). Yet if you know the backstory to Nehemiah, as told in 1 and 2 Kings, you realize that from the earliest days to the latest, from the North to the South, the children of Israel worshipped other gods. They worshipped the gods of their neighbors in the land—gods named Baal, Asherah, and Molech, among others. This started, in fact, even before there was a kingdom, when Moses was still up on the mountain receiving the laws and instructions from God. The people asked Aaron to make a god for them, and he made them a golden calf to worship (see Exodus 32). They thought that by worshipping these *other* gods along with the one true God, that it would give them a better chance of safety and prosperity. They thought that worshipping the other gods would bail them out, in case the Lord didn't come through for them. By worshipping the Lord *among* rather than *alone,* the Israelites believed that they would receive maximum protection from all possible divine powers.

Or they formed alliances with other kingdoms, which led to the worship of their gods. And sometimes the worship of these other gods involved temple prostitutes, who enticed some of the men to worship those gods. The people of Israel and Judah suffered from fear, insecurity, and illicit desire. And their solution throughout their history as a people was to run after what Don Henley called "little tin gods."

THEY DIDN'T HAVE AN IDOLATRY PROBLEM; THEY HAD AN IDOLATRY SOLUTION.

As I see the predicament that Judah is in at the beginning of Nehemiah—broken walls, burned gates, hollow spirits—I realize from Nehemiah's words *why* that all happened. Here's what hits me: The people of Judah and Jerusalem didn't have an idolatry problem;

they had an idolatry *solution*. Their problems had to do with fear, insecurity, unpopularity, lack of trust, and excess libido. But the solution they sought was what led them into exile and lingering shame upon their return.

I must tell you, in the twenty-first century, not much has changed. I see the same thing in myself. I had a sick day a while back and was just feeling rotten about myself, as if getting sick meant that I was somehow failing at my ministry. Makes total sense, right? Sickness equals failure or poor job performance. Of course, that's not true at all; but such was my thinking. Anyway, at the end of the day, I binged on a bag of gluten-free sweet potato chips. Now I realize: I didn't have a chip problem; I had a chip solution. Chips were my solution to my larger problem of irrational insecurity.

Many of us, if we are being honest with ourselves, will recognize that we do the same thing all too often. Some of us bounce from relationship to relationship to relationship, looking for something in a significant other that's always elusive. We always think that the next relationship will give us the fulfillment that we feel we lack. If that's you, I want you to realize now that you don't have a relationship *problem*; you have a relationship *solution*. For others, perhaps it has gone to the next level and involves jumping from one spouse to the next, hoping that the next one will be "right." Friends, that's not a marriage problem; it's a marriage solution. The same can be said for those who spend too much time on the Internet looking at certain websites. It's not a pornography problem, but a pornography solution. Some of us, perhaps, shop compulsively, chasing satisfaction through acquiring possessions. But again, that is not a shopping problem; it's a shopping solution. There are many, many situations to which we could apply this same logic.

I have even seen this type of thing happen in the church, where people confuse the problem for the solution. Some people will hop from church to church, or from leader to leader, or from author to author, always in search of the perfect version. But what's really going on is that they are trying to find in a person what only a living relationship with Jesus Christ can accomplish. It's not a church problem; it's a church solution. And there's a real, underlying problem that only the Lord of the church can provide.

Now, in all these instances I can't name the real problems with certainty. Often they have to do with parenting issues or personal insecurity, but they could be any number of things. Or perhaps they have to do with the subtle thought that God is not good. We don't trust that God really is good, so we choose something else instead. Yet even if I don't know the exact problems we face, I know for sure that the solutions we often identify for our problems aren't working. Whether we are like my friend at an open AA meeting, or we're living on the computer and drowning in credit card debt, we're often there because we turn to these things as our solutions. And these solutions can ruin our lives.

We've become problemists.

That is what Nehemiah realizes about himself and the people he is going to represent in Nehemiah 1:6-7. "We have wronged you greatly," Nehemiah says (verse 7). On behalf of his people, he repents of everything that they have done wrong. He turns away from all of the idolatry, all of the injustice, all of the lack of faith in the Lord.

And then Nehemiah's prayer takes a turn: "Remember the word that you gave to your servant Moses when you said, 'If you are unfaithful, I will scatter you among the peoples. But if you return to me and keep my commandments by really doing them, then, even though your outcasts live under distant skies, I will gather them from there and bring them to the place that I have chosen as a dwelling for my name'" (Nehemiah 1:8-9). He asks God to remember, as if God has somehow forgotten about the covenant and promise. Can you imagine being that nervy and confident with the Lord? Nehemiah asks God to remember God's own word, by which the people were scattered because they had been unfaithful (verse 8). That has happened, and Nehemiah is calling on God to remember the second part of God's word. If the people return to God, even if they are outcasts who "live under distant skies," God will bring them home. Even if they, like Nehemiah, are as far away as Susa, God will bring them home.

What a promise! The farthest the people could possibly wander from the presence of God—because of insecurity, fear, and false solutions—is still not too far from God's loving grasp. It's still not too far from God's welcome home. They're never too far, and it's never too late.

YOU'RE NEVER TOO FAR. IT'S NEVER TOO LATE.

That says everything to those of us for whom the solution has now become the problem. You're never too far. It's never too late. Your solution may have made you feel that your walls are broken and your gate is burnt and that you are *beyond* the distant skies, beyond farthest horizons. . . . But no. The promise God had given to Nehemiah and his people is a promise that still stands today. The faux solutions you've sought will never have the final word. Because here's what we get from Nehemiah's story and the backstory that Nehemiah draws upon: ***When you admit that the solution is the problem, God surrounds you with God's promises.***

Just look at the words Nehemiah ascribes to himself and his people (circle them) in verses 9-11: *gather; redeemed; success; favor; your people.* The tone of Nehemiah's expectations in his prayer changes dramatically from the present reality that he has heard about from his brother. Right now they are in "great trouble and shame," with broken walls and burned gates (verse 3). But Nehemiah says that they will be redeemed, be gathered, and be God's people. He prays for success and favor. And it all hinges on that "first step" he takes in verse 6: confession. We've blown it, he says to God. Our solution is really our problem. And God answers back with this deluge of promises.

When you turn away from false solutions and receive God's promises, they are like a breath of fresh air. It reminds me of a friend of mine who stopped drinking after years of abusing alcohol. What he said to me was, "Wow! I *feel* stuff now! I used to numb it all. Now I feel it all. Everything I feel isn't always good, but it is

WHEN YOU ADMIT THAT THE SOLUTION IS THE PROBLEM, GOD SURROUNDS YOU WITH GOD'S PROMISES.

21

always better than numb." When he gave up his problem-causing solution, he could receive everything that life had to offer him. *When you admit that the solution is the problem, God surrounds you with God's promises.* Or it's like the woman I know who used to cut herself. That was her solution, but she was able to give it up when she turned to Christ and let his promises surround her. When she at long last embraced that she was the blood-bought daughter of the king, she was able to stop spilling her own blood. *When you admit that the solution is the problem, God surrounds you with God's promises.* It's why I love that Christ-centered treatment center in New Jersey where the residents don't identify themselves by their addiction ("I'm John, and I'm an alcoholic."), but by their Savior: "I'm John; and I'm a blood-bought child of God, who already has victory over drugs." That's a promise worth savoring.

After Nehemiah confesses his people's sins, his prayer immediately turns to God's promises; he is moved to hope and action. Even Nehemiah's name points us toward God's promises. Do you know what *Nehemiah* means? *The Lord comforts.* Yes! Comfort comes not from our fake solutions, but from God. And God's promises will never fail us.

So, how is God challenging you? You know. Where is God dealing with you, letting you know that your solution is, in fact, your problem? Where have your solutions given you a broken wall and a burned gate? And where is God encouraging you to dig deeper, to peel back the onion of your own psyche, to see what the *real* problem is? Maybe it's a warped view of how others think about you, or a sneaking suspicion that God is not really, truly good— that God is not authentically enough. Sometimes our inability to embrace and celebrate how thoroughly we are *loved* makes us move on to idols. We can't accept God's tenacious grace. Oh, if that's you, just allow yourself to be surrounded by God's promises.

Speaking of which, let these promises surround you now:

> The mountains may shift,
>> and the hills may be shaken,
>> but my faithful love won't shift from you,
>> and my covenant of peace won't be shaken,
>> says the LORD, the one who pities you. (Isaiah 54:10)

> Your kingdom is a kingship that lasts forever;
>> your rule endures for all generations.
> The LORD is trustworthy in all that he says,
>> faithful in all that he does. (Psalm 145:13)

So what are we going to say about these things? If God is for us, who is against us? He didn't spare his own Son but gave him up for us all. Won't he also freely give us all things with him? (Romans 8:31-32)

"Come to me, all you who are struggling hard and carrying heavy loads, and I will give you rest. Put on my yoke, and learn from me. I'm gentle and humble. And you will find rest for yourselves. My yoke is easy to bear, and my burden is light." (Matthew 11:28-30)

Questions for Reflection and Discussion

Write responses and other thoughts in the space below each question. If you are discussing the book in a small group, prepare for the meeting by writing answers in advance.

1. What did you know about Nehemiah before this study? How did the explanation of the backstory above help you understand Nehemiah better?

2. Nehemiah seems to be pretty certain that his people's troubles are due to their sin. How does this perspective challenge you or encourage you?

3. What hope do you see in Nehemiah's prayer? What is the source of his hope?

4. How can we have a similar source of hope in our own lives and in our world?

5. Where have you seen people confuse problems and solutions? In those cases, what tend to be the underlying problems that led them to pursue false solutions?

6. Do you have any broken gates or burnt walls today? How did you get there, and how is God seeking to make repairs in you or through you?

7. Which of the promises of God do you hang on to with the most fervor? How do they sustain you?

Turn to God's Promises

What do you need to confess, like Nehemiah did? Spend some time in introspection this week, asking God to open your eyes to any false solutions, any things you turn to for help or healing that will create only more problems for you. How can you turn, instead, to God's promises?

Closing Prayer

O Lord, thank you for opening our eyes and pulling back the veil on all of the phony solutions that we run after. Thank you for this reminder that you really are good and trustworthy. No matter how far we go from you, we are never too far and it's never too late. Thank you for reaching out to pull us back even today. Fill us with grace to stop pursuing our own solutions and turn to you, to be surrounded and upheld by your promises. Amen.

Daily Scripture Readings

Monday: 2 Kings 17–18
Tuesday: 2 Kings 19–20
Wednesday: 2 Kings 21–22
Thursday: 2 Kings 23–24
Friday: 2 Kings 25

LET'S DO THIS!

*I went out by night ... so that I could inspect the walls of
Jerusalem that had been broken down, as well as its gates, which had
been destroyed by fire. (Nehemiah 2:13)*

I bet this happens in your life because I know that it happens
in mine. Somewhere in your house—or your workplace, or
your car—stuff collects. For me, it's the garage. Things just
seem to collect in my garage. And in my case, the "stuff" is
usually little slips of paper: receipts, notes, or cards that somehow
fall out of the car and onto the floor of the garage. The first couple
of times I see these slips of paper lying there, I choose not to do
anything about it. I'm in a hurry, or I'm cold, or I'm trying to evade
the cat. And I think, "Well, I'll just get that later." And then *later*
turns into *never*; eventually, I stop seeing it altogether. I get used to
it. The dirt, the paper, or whatever other mess simply becomes part
of the garage scenery. I stop noticing what shouldn't be there, and I
come to regard it as part of what should. Eventually, paper and mess
covers the floor of the garage; and it's all but invisible to me.

I know that I'm not the only one who does this. In some ways, it's human nature. It's why you have piles of useless stuff in your house, why your workspace is out of alignment, why your car doubles as a closet, and why even the tidiest person alive has a place *somewhere* in his or her life that is cluttered, crumbling, messy. It's not this way because we like the mess. It's because we have gotten used to it. We have come to accept it.

This happens more than in the garage, or the house, or the car, or the closet. It happens in life. We get used to things that shouldn't be there. We *settle*. It's one of the saddest things for me to observe as pastor, when people get used to having stuff in their selves or their relationships that they should actually never tolerate. But I see it happen far too often, because, as novelist Anthony Abbot says, life stops hurting so much when you give up dreaming that it could be any different.

WE GET USED TO THINGS THAT SHOULDN'T BE THERE.

I've seen it happen with abuse, where people have gotten used to the verbal, psychological, or even physical abuse that happens in their households. Or I've seen it happen the other way, where people become accustomed to doling out the abuse. They've gotten used to expressing their vitriol much too freely, with no filter between their thoughts and their words. Others have gotten used to addictive behavior in themselves or in their family. Either they're the ones who indulge in it ("just a little!") or the ones who enable it. It's easy to justify the behavior so that it becomes a part of one's life. Or it's just easier to coexist than to deal with it; so all in all, one gets used to it. It happens in the professional world as well. Sometimes people who lead at work actually get used to low-performers. They settle into an equilibrium in which it is easier to coexist and compensate for what should be considered unacceptable performance. In all of these instances, something is out of place. Something is wrong, making a mess; but you get used to it, and so it stays. Eventually, it just becomes part of the scenery.

In my own world, there was a period of time during which I had settled as a pastor. Until about eight years ago or so, I had settled on a method of sermon design that was simple but had become stale. It was easy and familiar, and it was all I knew; but it wasn't as effective as it could have been. I had just gotten used to it.

Actually, whole churches get used to all kinds of stuff that they shouldn't tolerate. I remember, early on in my tenure at a church, an apparently trusted, wise leader took me aside for a little history lesson. He told how in 1984, he'd had to arrange for the pastor at the time to leave the church. And then a little later, in 1988, he'd had to engineer another departure, when it was time for the next pastor to leave. And then again, in 1990, he'd had to do the same thing to the pastor after that. And now here I was, the new pastor; and he and I were fine. I tucked that info away and thought, "OK, history noted. But, of course, I'll be different; he'll always love me!" But of course that wasn't the case. Six years later, he told me it was time for me to leave that church. (His logic was that Jesus only stayed on earth for three and a half years, and then his humanity started to "show out." That's why United Methodist pastors should move every 3–4 years.) I, of course, stayed two more years just to show him that he didn't have that kind of clout. But you know what the people in the church said about him? "Oh, that's just so-and-so. We're used to that from him." That's like just getting used to an

infection that's destroying your health. In 2015, I discovered that
the same man was at it again twenty-five years later. He'd changed
churches, but not patterns; he is in leadership at another church
and trying to fire their pastor. The funny thing for me is, he says it's
the pastor's time to go because that guy is trying to make his church
just like Good Shepherd! Go figure. It's almost comical, but it's not.
Because another church has gotten used to something that should
have never been allowed in the first place.

All of this brings us back to the Book of Nehemiah, which is
our ground for exploring God's solutions in this book. As a brief
reminder of the scenario, remember that the Book of Nehemiah
is set in 445 B.C. The man Nehemiah is living in the lap of luxury
in Persia (modern-day Iran), serving the Persian king Ataxerxes.
Nehemiah himself is a Jew; and in the first chapter of the book,
he gets a report about Jerusalem, the city of his people and his
ancestry. He has most likely never even visited Jerusalem; but from
the report, he learns that the city is in ruins. The Babylonians had
ransacked it about 150 years earlier; its protective walls are still
broken, and its gates are still burned (Nehemiah 1:3). For some
reason, immediately upon receiving the report, Nehemiah knows
what he must do: He must go to Jerusalem to rebuild the city. In
Nehemiah chapter 2, he begins to take action. Let's take a look at
what happens:

> [1] In the month of Nisan, in the twentieth year of King
> Artaxerxes, the king was about to be served wine. I took the
> wine and gave it to the king. Since I had never seemed sad
> in his presence, [2] the king asked me, "Why do you seem sad?
> Since you aren't sick, you must have a broken heart!"
>
> I was very afraid [3] and replied, "May the king live forever!
> Why shouldn't I seem sad when the city, the place of my
> family's graves, is in ruins and its gates destroyed by fire?"

⁴The king asked, "What is it that you need?"

I prayed to the God of heaven ⁵and replied, "If it pleases the king, and if your servant has found favor with you, please send me to Judah, to the city of my family's graves so that I may rebuild it."

⁶With the queen sitting beside him, the king asked me, "How long will you be away and when will you return?" So it pleased the king to send me, and I told him how long I would be gone.

⁷I also said to him, "If it pleases the king, may letters be given me addressed to the governors of the province Beyond the River to allow me to travel to Judah. ⁸May the king also issue a letter to Asaph the keeper of the king's forest, directing him to supply me with timber for the beams of the temple fortress gates, for the city wall, and for the house in which I will live."

The king gave me what I asked, for the gracious power of my God was with me.

⁹So I went to the governors of the province Beyond the River and gave them the king's letters. The king had sent officers of the army and cavalry with me.

¹⁰When Sanballat the Horonite and Tobiah the Ammonite official heard this, they were very angry that someone had come to seek the welfare of the people of Israel.

¹¹When I reached Jerusalem and had been there for three days, ¹²I set out at night, taking only a few people with me. I didn't tell anyone what my God was prompting me to do for Jerusalem, and the only animal I took was the one I rode. ¹³I went out by night through the Valley Gate past the Dragon's Spring to the Dung Gate so that I could inspect the

walls of Jerusalem that had been broken down, as well as its gates, which had been destroyed by fire.

[14] Then I went on to the Spring Gate and to the King's Pool. Since there was no room for the animal on which I was riding to pass, [15] I went up by way of the valley by night and inspected the wall. Then I turned back and returned by entering through the Valley Gate.

[16] The officials didn't know where I had gone or what I was doing. I hadn't yet told the Jews, the priests, the officials, the officers, or the rest who were to do the work. [17] So I said to them, "You see the trouble that we're in: Jerusalem is in ruins, and its gates are destroyed by fire! Come, let's rebuild the wall of Jerusalem so that we won't continue to be in disgrace." [18] I told them that my God had taken care of me, and also told them what the king had said to me.

"Let's start rebuilding!" they said, and they eagerly began the work.

[19] But when Sanballat the Horonite, Tobiah the Ammonite official, and Geshem the Arab heard about it, they mocked and made fun of us. "What are you doing?" they asked. "Are you rebelling against the king?"

[20] "The God of heaven will give us success!" I replied. "As God's servants, we will start building. But you will have no share, right, or claim in Jerusalem."

Nehemiah approaches the Persian king and asks him for permission to go and rebuild the walls and gates of Jerusalem. Notice Nehemiah's references to "my family" in verses 3 and 5. Nehemiah is in King Artaxerxes' service, and he lives many miles away from Jerusalem. But his connection to the city runs deep because it runs through his family. It runs through his history. Nehemiah is a part of the people of God; and because the city of

God is in ruins, the name of God is in disgrace. That is Nehemiah's motivation for wanting to travel to Jerusalem to rebuild it.

So after working up all kinds of divine courage through prayer (verse 4), Nehemiah asks the king to send him from Susa to Jerusalem. The journey was hundreds of miles, and it would have taken him many months just to get there. As it turns out, Nehemiah ends up staying in Jerusalem for twelve years, which is very likely a good deal longer than the visit Artaxerxes had in mind. But at the outset, knowing how long Nehemiah anticipated being gone (see verse 6), the king allows him to go. And then Nehemiah goes a step further, asking Artaxerxes to send official letters recognizing Nehemiah's mission and supplying materials for the building project (verses 7-8). Nehemiah begins his task of rebuilding Jerusalem with full royal support, because God was with him (verse 8).

Remember, Jerusalem is the place of Nehemiah's ancestry, but it's also a place he himself has likely never laid eyes on before. So when Nehemiah gets to Jerusalem, he needs to do some reconnaissance to understand the extent of the destruction and the repairs that are needed. And this is exactly what he does, three days after his arrival in Jerusalem (Nehemiah 2:11-15). The catch, though, is that Nehemiah does this in secret: "I set out at night, taking only a few people with me. I didn't tell anyone what my God was prompting me to do for Jerusalem, and the only animal I took was the one I rode" (Nehemiah 2:12). Nehemiah kept his plan to himself, hiding his actions under the cover of night. He knew that were anyone to learn of his plan to repair and rebuild what had been crumbled for so long, it would have started all kinds of trouble before he had started any kind of repair.

Conducting his survey under the cover of darkness must not have been easy. But despite his need for secrecy, Nehemiah performed a thorough inspection of the city walls and gates. Listen to his meticulous account of his inspection in verses 13-15: "I went out by night through the Valley Gate past the Dragon's Spring to the Dung Gate so that I could inspect the walls of Jerusalem that had been broken down, as well as its gates, which had been destroyed by fire. Then I went on to the Spring Gate and to the King's Pool. Since there was no room for the animal on which I was riding to pass, I went up by way of the valley by night and inspected the wall. Then I turned back and returned by entering through the Valley Gate."

NEHEMIAH MAKES A CAREFUL INSPECTION, NOTING WHAT'S WRONG AND OUT OF PLACE DOWN TO THE LAST DETAIL.

Now, can we acknowledge that examining the "Dung Gate" doesn't sound very appealing? Not exactly anybody's dream job! But the word that really stands out to me is the word *inspect* in verses 13 and 15. Another translation uses the word *examine* (NIV). The word means a careful investigation, a close inspection or examination of Jerusalem's walls and gates. Nehemiah is so meticulous. He surveys and catalogs the damage to the once-strong gate and once-strong city walls. He takes the time to see and record what others have gotten used to. I have to think that the residents of Jerusalem had ceased to notice the burned gates and broken walls, much as I so often cease to notice the paper strewn about on my garage floor. But Nehemiah makes a careful inspection, noting what's wrong and out of place, down to the very last detail of every gate and every section of the wall. It would be like someone going through my garage and carefully noting the location of every last receipt, sticky note, or scrap of paper that I'd allowed to build up on the floor. Nehemiah goes in and, despite the necessity for secrecy, takes inventory of what's wrong with Jerusalem.

Nehemiah's fresh eyes are able to record what the people of the city had become numb to. The Jews living in the midst of their clutter and failure had given up dreaming that life could be any different. They had *settled*. They had gotten used to their mess, and you never get rid of what you get used to. Whether it's a garage in Charlotte in 2016 or a wall in Jerusalem in 445 B.C., the truth is the same: If you get used to it, you don't get rid of it. Nehemiah's reconnaissance was the fresh eyes that the people of Jerusalem needed to point out what they should not have tolerated.

LET'S START REBUILDING!

After his inspection, Nehemiah tells the leaders of the city his plans: "So I said to them, 'You see the trouble that we're in: Jerusalem is in ruins, and its gates are destroyed by fire! Come, let's rebuild the wall of Jerusalem so that we won't continue to be in disgrace'" (Nehemiah 2:17). The best word in Nehemiah's speech is *we're*—as in "we are." Nehemiah doesn't use the word *I*, but *we*. He is one of them, one of the people of Jerusalem. Even though he has been in that place for only about five days, after growing up hundreds of miles away, Nehemiah regards himself as one of them. Because of ancestry, because of history, and because of his connection to God, it takes him only five days to become a

YOU GET RID OF ONLY WHAT YOU REFUSE TO GET USED TO.

Jerusalemite. This means that his inspection of the city was not for his benefit only but for the benefit of all the citizens. His inspection opened not only his eyes but theirs as well, enabling them to see the damage they'd gotten used to.

The people's enthusiastic response to Nehemiah's plan shows that he truly had opened their eyes: "Let's start rebuilding!" (Nehemiah 2:18). They're on board. They suddenly see the evidence of Jerusalem's disgrace and decide to stop tolerating it. They begin the work "eagerly" (verse 18), committing themselves to get rid of the disgrace that they had gotten used to. And the rest of Nehemiah's memoir is exactly that story, how Nehemiah mobilizes the people for ministry and productivity. If we are to pursue God's solutions in a world of problems the way that Nehemiah did, here is what we can learn from his example: *You get rid of only what you refuse to get used to.*

I can hardly tell you how much I believe this or how vital I think it is in both individual and organizational lives. I believe it so much because I've lived it. In 2010, we who made up the leadership of Good Shepherd Church felt as though we'd been plateauing for a few years; so we brought in some fresh eyes in the form of a consultant. Even though we didn't know it at the time, he turned out to be our modern-day Nehemiah. He inspected our walls and gates every bit as thoroughly as Nehemiah had inspected Jerusalem. He opened our eyes to all of the things that we had gotten used to, all of the things that were wrong but that we no longer saw anymore.

He helped us see, for instance, that we were "branding the bullet but not the gun," meaning that we had great sermon series; but the church as a whole lacked direction. He helped us see that some of our signage in the parking lot was confusing at best and unwelcoming at worst. He showed us how our exterior wall space was largely empty, and he opened our eyes to ways this space could be used to fulfill our mission. For us, the exterior wall space was simply how our church building looked. The parking lot signs were just part of the scenery, and we'd been around them enough to stop seeing them as visitors did.

This modern-day Nehemiah opened our eyes to the things we needed to refuse to get used to, and we were able to get rid of them. We changed our signage to be more visitor friendly and helpful. We used our exterior wall space to display a banner that told people who we are at Good Shepherd and what we are about. And while our sermon series are still pretty good, they all serve the church's larger mission of "inviting all people into a living relationship with Jesus Christ." Everything we do now supports that mission; it gives us direction and guides us toward our purpose. It's all because that modern-day Nehemiah helped us see all of the harmful stuff that we had settled for and learned to coexist with. *You get rid of only what you refuse to get used to.*

An important step in twelve-step recovery programs goes like this: "We made a searching and fearless moral inventory of ourselves." I love that. It's really a way of saying that as part of addiction recovery, you take a merciless magnifying glass to look at your own stuff. It's doing the work in your own life that Nehemiah did with Jerusalem's gates and walls. It's taking note of every broken down wall or burned-out gate, everything that is out of place in your own heart and life, so that you can begin to make repairs.

So I have to ask: What about *you* have you gotten used to? What is the stuff that clutters up your life, stuff that you should never have tolerated but you have stopped noticing? Is it smoking? Habitual laziness? Cutting off your mind via video entertainment? Selfishness? Anger? Or maybe it's something you have gotten used to in your relationships with others. Have you gotten used to someone's complaining, or inattentiveness, or lack of affection? Have you gotten used to your own personal insecurity? Where in your life have you settled? What is needed for you to open your eyes and notice the clutter so that you can stop getting used to it and start getting rid of it?

WHAT HAVE YOU GOTTEN USED TO?

Even in your living relationship with Jesus Christ, what have you gotten used to? Perhaps you have come to terms with your own ignorance of the Bible, just telling yourself that it's the way things are. Or maybe you've stopped praying as much or stopped praying altogether, and you've stopped feeling that pull to strengthen your connected with God through prayer. Or have you gotten used to a solitary spiritual life rather than one that's supported by the community of other believers? Living in isolation rather than community? Whatever it is, I want to challenge you to take a spiritual, personal inventory of yourself and then gauge how much are you wanting, pursuing, longing for Jesus in every aspect of your life. My prayer for everyone reading this is that you would inspect your own life as carefully as Nehemiah examined that wall. Because *you get rid of only what you refuse to get used to.*

We can undertake this inventory with confidence and trust, in the same spirit that Nehemiah undertook his inspection of Jerusalem. He could do this fearlessly and thoroughly, because he had God on his side. Look at what he tells the leaders and officials of Jerusalem when he tells them of his plan: "I told them that my God had taken care of me, and also told them what the king had said to me" (Nehemiah 2:18). Nehemiah has royal backing; but more than that, he has God's favor. God has taken care of him, and so he trusts that God will watch over his work in rebuilding Jerusalem. Nehemiah is able to be so ruthless in seeing what's true because he knows that he is operating under the favor of God. You might say that Nehemiah is like a professional wrestler. Newsflash: The outcome of a pro wrestling match is never in doubt. The winner is predetermined. A pro wrestler doesn't fight *for* victory; he fights *from* victory. Fighting from victory changes how you go about your business in the ring. And Nehemiah's connection to and faith in God was so deep, so sure, so rooted in history and ancestry, that he knew the results before they ever came to pass. As you undertake the difficult personal, professional, or even congregational inventory and inspection, may you do so also in the assurance that God will empower you to get rid of what you've gotten used to.

Questions for Reflection and Discussion

Write responses and other thoughts in the space below each question. If you are discussing the book in a small group, prepare for the meeting by writing answers in advance.

1. Why did Nehemiah conduct his inspection of Jerusalem's wall and gates at night?

2. Why do the leaders and officials in Jerusalem respond so positively to Nehemiah's proposal to rebuild the city walls? What sorts of thoughts or emotions might they have experienced?

3. What is it about Nehemiah that empowers him to get so many people on his side?

4. How would you characterize Nehemiah's leadership, based on what you have seen in Nehemiah 1–2? What about him inspires you?

5. In your mind's eye, go through your home and your work place. What have you gotten used to in these spaces that probably doesn't belong?

6. Now consider your behaviors and relationships. What have you tolerated in yourself or in your relationships that threatens to dominate you or hold you back?

7. What would it take for you to notice the clutter that you have gotten used to? What would it mean for you to get rid of these things?

Inspect Your Walls

Make a careful inspection of your own personal life this week, taking note of the broken walls or burned gates within yourself or your relationships. Open your eyes and try to notice all of the things you have gotten used to that really shouldn't be there. Ask for God's grace to show you these things and to help free you from them so that you might grow in your living relationship with Jesus Christ.

Closing Prayer

Eternal God, we thank you for Nehemiah's willingness to make a careful inspection of all of the repairs that were needed in Jerusalem. We thank you for the example it shows all of us who have gotten used to something, who have settled because we've stopped dreaming that life could be any different. Give us fresh eyes to see. Give us the courage of our ancestor Nehemiah to take a close look at our own lives and the world around us. And guide us to respond to the challenges that we uncover. Amen.

Daily Scripture Readings

Monday: 2 Chronicles 29
Tuesday: 2 Chronicles 33
Wednesday: 2 Chronicles 34–35
Thursday: 2 Chronicles 36:1-14
Friday: 2 Chronicles 36:15-23

3

FOOD NETWORK SOLUTIONS

I was very angry when I heard their protest and these complaints. After thinking it over, I brought charges against the officials and the officers. (Nehemiah 5:6-7a)

What moves you? There are some situations that have the ability to stir up powerful emotions, making us either supernaturally buoyant or righteously indignant. These are the things that move us to tears. For instance, there's the fight song from Southern Methodist University that stirs up emotions in me. I didn't even go to SMU. But my father taught there; and I grew up in Dallas, literally in the shadow of that school. We even played a part of the fight song at my dad's funeral. So every time I hear that song, I am filled with nostaligia. It simply moves me. There's also the song *One Shining Moment,* with tournament highlights, that they play at the end of college basketball's March Madness every year. And of course, my emotions are stirred by Jim Valvano's words, which became the motto of his foundation to combat cancer: "Don't give up. Don't ever give up." And lest you think I have an emotional response to only college basketball, let me tell you that I am also deeply moved by Martin Luther King Jr.'s "I Have a Dream" speech and by Ronald Reagan's words about the Berlin wall: "Mr. Gorbachev, tear down this wall!" These things move me, stirring up my emotions and giving me inspiration.

There are other things, too, that move us in a different way. They stir up righteous indignation in us, causing to feel not inspired or uplifted, but sympathetic or even angry. Think about how you feel when your team is cheated in a sporting event, or when someone you care about receives unfair treatment. It's the same way you feel when you see a documentary about human trafficking or people living in abject poverty somewhere in the world. It's the way your emotions are engaged when you hear about the latest atrocity by ISIS. When you see a child abandoned. When you see a pet abused. In those situations and many others like them, your passions rise and your adrenaline flows—but in an altogether different direction than the things that uplift us. These things make us angry and challenge us, because we know that things like them should not happen in our world.

The challenge when we encounter circumstances that move us is: How do we translate our inward movement into outward action? Many such circumstances call out for some kind of intervention, some type of restitution. And if we are people who pursue God's solutions, we must embrace this call for action.

This is precisely what Nehemiah does when he confronts a situation in Jerusalem that moves him to righteous anger. His response can guide us as we confront similar situations today.

By way of reminder, here is the background of Nehemiah: In 445 B.C., Nehemiah received word that Jerusalem, the city of his ancestors, was in ruins. Its gates were burned and its walls were broken down. The city had been in this sort of condition for a century and a half, as the Babylonians had destroyed it in 587 B.C. Even though Nehemiah lived hundreds of miles away from Jerusalem, he traveled to the city to undertake the reconstruction of the wall. In the last chapter, we saw how Nehemiah inspected and examined the ruins and then mobilized the city's residents to begin reconstruction.

In the middle of their flurry of activity, however, a secondary problem crops up. (Isn't that the way it *always* works? You work hard to fix one thing; and in that process, something completely different breaks.) Nehemiah chapter 5 tells the story of the hardship that Nehemiah's people encounter, and how Nehemiah responds to it:

> [1] Then there was a great protest of the people and their wives against their fellow Jews. [2] Some said, "With our sons and daughters we are many, and we all need grain to eat and stay alive."
>
> [3] Others said, "We have to mortgage our fields, our vineyards, and our houses in order to get grain during the famine."
>
> [4] Still others said, "We have had to borrow money against our fields and vineyards in order to pay the king's tax."
>
> [5] "We are of the same flesh and blood as our kin, and our children are the same as theirs. Yet we are just about to force our sons and daughters into slavery, and some of our daughters are already slaves! There is nothing we can do since our fields and vineyards now belong to others."
>
> [6] I was very angry when I heard their protest and these complaints. [7] After thinking it over, I brought charges against the officials and the officers. I told them, "You are all taking interest from your own people!" I also called for a large assembly in order to deal with them. [8] "To the best of our ability," I said to them, "we have bought back our Jewish

kin who had been sold to other nations. But now you are selling your own kin, who must then be bought back by us!" At this they were silent, unable to offer a response.

⁹ So I continued, "What you are doing isn't good! Why don't you walk in the fear of our God? This will prevent the taunts of the nations that are our enemies! ¹⁰ I myself, along with my family and my servants, am lending them money and grain. But let's stop charging this interest! ¹¹ Give it back to them, right now. Return their fields, their vineyards, their olive orchards, and their houses. And give back the interest on money, grain, wine, and oil that you are charging them."

¹² They replied, "We'll return everything, and we won't charge anything else. We'll do what you've asked."

So I called the priests and made them swear to do what they had promised. ¹³ I also shook out the fold of my robe, saying, "So may God shake out everyone from their house and property if they don't keep this promise. So may they be shaken out and emptied!"

The whole assembly said, "Amen," and praised the Lord. And the people did as they had promised.

¹⁴ In addition, from the time that I was appointed to be their governor in the land of Judah (that is, from the twentieth to the thirty-second year of King Artaxerxes for a total of twelve years), neither I nor my family ate from the governor's food allowance. ¹⁵ The earlier governors who had come before me laid heavy burdens on the people. They took food and wine from them as well as forty shekels of silver. Even their servants oppressed the people. But because I was God-fearing, I didn't behave in this way.

¹⁶ Instead, I devoted myself to the work on this wall. We acquired no land, and all my servants were gathered there

for the work. [17] One hundred fifty Jews and officials, along with those who came to us from the surrounding nations, gathered around my table. [18] One ox, six choice sheep, and birds were prepared each day. Every ten days there was a large amount of wine. Yet even with this I didn't ask for the governor's food allowance because of the heavy burden the people had to carry.

[19] Remember in my favor, my God, all that I've done for this people!

The people brought this new problem to Nehemiah by way of a "great protest" (verse 1) in Nehemiah 5:1-5. They had already been facing hardship in the form of opposition to their work (see Nehemiah 4). But then Nehemiah discovered that their most basic needs for survival were not being met. A lot of the people working on the wall had taken time away from their family farms to help Nehemiah rebuild the wall, and this led to a lack of food. "With our sons and daughters we are many, and we all need grain to eat and stay alive" (Nehemiah 5:2). Solidarity and cooperation on the wall's construction was one thing; but with no one to work the farms, the families in question were left without a way to secure food. On top of that, verse 3 mentions a famine that had hit Jerusalem, compounding the problem.

Worst of all, however, was the social and economic inequality, which led to abuse. Many of the people had to borrow money against their fields, vineyards, and houses just to have food to eat. Others had to do the same thing so that they could afford to pay the taxes they owed the king (Nehemiah 5:3-4). They were on the brink of selling their own children into slavery; and for some this had already begun (verse 5). But the real injustice comes at the beginning of verse 5: "We are of the same flesh and blood as our kin…." *Our kin. Same flesh and blood.* Here was this beleaguered minority community just trying to get back on its feet, and they were cheating one another. The wealthy few among them were taking advantage of the circumstances to increase their wealth at the expense of their own people. There was a duel between the haves and the have-nots; predictably, the haves were winning. Their victory came through charging usurious interest rates. The haves took advantage of their oh-so-vulnerable kinsfolk by offering sub-prime mortgages cluttered up by confusing loan documents, and the result was a mass of foreclosures.

The irony, in 445 B.C., was that this was exactly the kind of mistreatment of the poor that led to the Babylonian exile a century and a half earlier, which was when the wall was torn down in the first place. So even though the exile was over and they had been brought home, they were repeating the same sinful oppression that got them punished in the first place. All in all, the whole situation was a huge mess: Nehemiah came to rebuild a wall and repair gates, but he soon found that he had to remedy the injustice within the community of Jerusalem's residents. If he did not, he might soon have to quell a rebellion.

Beginning in verse 6, Nehemiah responds: "I was very angry when I heard their protest and these complaints." *I was very angry*. You know what that means? Nehemiah was *moved* by these circumstances. He heard the cries, he assessed the situation, and he felt the mess of the people. His emotions were touched, and his adrenaline began to pump. His reaction was much like yours when you when you read about human trafficking, or when you see starving children have distended bellies, or when you see an innocent person mistreated. He was moved.

What interests me most, though, is what Nehemiah did next. In the very next verse, he acts: "After thinking it over, I brought charges against the officials and the officers" (Nehemiah 5:7). Nehemiah

NEHEMIAH MOVES QUICKLY FROM FEELING TO THOUGHT TO ACTION.

moved quickly from feeling to thought to action. He became angry, he considered his options, and then he did something about it. The way verse 7 is worded, we get the impression that Nehemiah's next step required only the briefest of reflections. He didn't need to study, to analyze, or—dare I say it—even to pray. He did enough thinking and consideration to understand what to do, and then he did it. He used his unique powers of persuasion and his position of authority to call those who were abusing the system to a better way. He told them that the usury they were charging was not good and that they should remember their blood relationship to their fellow Jews. He persuaded them to give back the fields, vineyards, olive orchards, and houses to those who had defaulted on their loans, and to return the high interest they had charged (verse 11). Remarkably, the people agreed to this; they returned what they had gained through interest and agreed to stop charging it when they lent to their fellow Jews (verse 12).

This strikes me as so different from our normal response to things that move us to righteous anger. What do we typically do? Might we establish a study committee? My fellow Methodists will recognize that as an all-too-familiar first step. Or perhaps we would set up a campaign to raise awareness. Build a website to call attention to the problem. Set up a think tank to study the issue further. Or begin a prayer vigil on behalf of those who are suffering. None of these are necessarily bad steps to take, but often they hold us back from taking truly meaningful action to fix the

MOVE ON WHAT YOU ARE MOVED BY.

problems we face. We can become so stymied by getting the word out or overthinking a problem that we neglect to do things that would make a real difference.

Nehemiah behaved differently. He acted to stop usury, to return property and livelihood, to start feeding. He acted to make the changes they needed to make in order to fix the situation. And what I love most is the short distance from emotion to action, from feeling to doing, from indignation to correction, from diagnosis to delivery. Nehemiah was moved deeply by the plight of the hungry, vulnerable Jews. But he didn't stop with the anger he felt. He moved on what he was moved by. And that's the idea today for all of us who wish to follow Nehemiah's example in pursuing God's solutions: *Move on what you are moved by.*

Nehemiah didn't raise awareness. He raised an army. He didn't wring his hands. He opened them. He didn't just feel sympathy. He embodied helpfulness. There was such a short synapse between what he felt and what he did, and that brevity summarizes his whole genius. He provides us with a powerful example to follow in addressing the problems we face in today's world.

When I preached a version of this chapter at Good Shepherd Church as part of our Solutionists series, we did our best to follow Nehemiah's example. We were in the early phases of our own construction and expansion project (which involved walls!), but it didn't mean that other issues in our community went away. Charlotte is a wonderful city, with beautiful buildings, big banks, and a good football team. But it also has people who are hungry, just like Jerusalem in Nehemiah's day. And Nehemiah inspired us to recognize that they deserved more than our *sympathy*; they required our *generosity*.

I brought in a guest that Sunday, Sue Bruce from Loaves & Fishes, a local organization that works to provide food for hungry people in the Charlotte area. She told our congregation about the hard realities of hunger that many people in Charlotte face. In Mecklenburg county alone, Loaves & Fishes fed almost eighty thousand people in 2014. A crowd that size would fill Bank of America Stadium, where the Carolina Panthers play football. That gave us an idea of how many hungry people lived in the Charlotte area. And forty-eight percent of those people were children. She went on to say that one in four children in the state of North Carolina are considered food-insecure, meaning that they sometimes do not know where their next meal will come from.

Sue Bruce also helped us understand the nature of hunger in our area. For many people who work in our city and state, low wages lead to extremely tight budgets. A single event, from a car repair to a sick child, can lead to an unexpected expense or cause them to lose hours—and pay—at work. This puts them in the difficult position of choosing whether to eat or to pay a bill or to purchase medicine. It really does sometimes become a choice between paying the rent or eating a meal.

> # OUR SYMPATHY NEVER FEEDS A SINGLE PERSON; OUR GENEROSITY DOES.

After our guest told us about hunger in the Charlotte area, I challenged the people of Good Shepherd with the following message: Our sympathy never feeds a single person. Our emotional reactions do not provide food. Our compassion doesn't fill plates. Our adrenaline doesn't pour glasses. Our awareness and righteous anger don't give food to those who need it. Our *generosity* does. We might judge ourselves by our thoughts and feelings and intentions. But hungry people evaluate us based on our actions.

Our goal that Sunday was not to raise awareness but to raise an army. Not to wring hands but to open them. And that's what we did. We challenged the people to take my brief sermon and our guest's brief conversation and turn it into action. Working with Loaves & Fishes and the scouting ministry at Good Shepherd, we handed out empty grocery bags with instructions on them. Everyone who took a grocery bag would bring it back the next Sunday filled with food. That's it. Simple. The instructions on each bag gave clear guidelines on what food was needed. It was not easy on everyone, but it was simple to execute. It did not take a lot of reflection, but it was saturated in action. We didn't start a campaign, didn't go door-to-door with information. We certainly didn't hold a committee meeting to discuss our best response as a congregation. Like Nehemiah, we wanted to *do* something, to shorten the distance between our sympathy and our actions. We didn't ask people to feel compassion or righteous anger; we asked them to put feet and hands to the compassion they already had. We challenged them to move on what they were moved by.

I want to challenge you with the same message today. Your sympathy won't feed, clothe, or shelter a single person. But your generosity will. So *move on what you are moved by*.

Nehemiah realized the crucial connection among the people who lived in Jerusalem. They were all the same flesh and blood; they were all the same family by virtue of their identity as Jews. And a similar connection exists between you and the people who are in need around you in your own communities. You are related to the people around you; they are your same flesh and blood. Many of them are Christians, and they are your brothers and sisters in Christ. And as for those who are not, they are still children of God. And so many of them are victims of forces beyond their control, in need of help. Maybe it's food. Maybe it's clothing. Maybe it's shelter. Or maybe it's something intangible, such as emotional support or someone to believe in them and invest in them with time and energy. And just like Nehemiah, we too can ask how we can allow our own people to suffer like this. Like Nehemiah, we can become angry. And we can do something. You know what it is that moves you. Move on it. *Move on what you are moved by*.

THE PEOPLE AROUND YOU ARE YOUR SAME FLESH AND BLOOD.

Nehemiah recognizes that God's very name is at stake in the condition of God's people. He knows that "the taunts of the nations" might well be aroused if God's people continue to oppress one another so that some of them go hungry (Nehemiah 5:9). When the people of God are hungry and marginalized, then the name of God is as well. When the people of God prey on one another, then the reputation of God diminishes. But the flip side is that when God's people shorten the distance between diagnosis and delivery, when they stop wringing their hands and start opening them, then the fame of God grows. When God's people choose generosity and provide for those in need, God's very name will be known and magnified by our actions. *Move on what you are moved by.*

When we challenged the people of Good Shepherd to move and act on the problem of hunger in the Charlotte area, they responded in a powerful way that truly glorified the name of God. Our congregation donated a total of 15,368 pounds of food, the second-largest in-kind donation they had received from a non-corporate donor and the largest in-kind donation they had ever received from a congregation. You'd better believe I was happy to be a part of that, to the glory of God.

The bottom line in the twenty-first century is the same as in 445 B.C.: We can pursue God's solutions by translating feeling and thinking into action. It's amazing what a difference our actions can make when God takes them and shapes them and works through them. I'm sure that even Nehemiah didn't anticipate the full turnaround he witnessed among the leaders and officials of the people when he confronted them about their high interest charges and unfair practices. But God was with him, and his efforts led to a true transformation in the community living in Jerusalem.

In the same way, when we provide food for the hungry, we will be amazed at the way God works through our generosity. I once heard a story about orphans who had been through a shocking amount of trauma during the Second World War. Although they were well fed at their orphanage, they could not sleep well at night. They'd been through so much trauma and uncertainty, and they were restless and afraid. Someone had an idea: They could give each child a piece of bread to sleep with at night—not to eat but to hold. (Now, if a child was hungry and ate it, another piece of bread would be provided.) The results were astonishing. The children began to rest peacefully. The sensation of holding the bread gave them a sense of security and hope, as if to reassure them that they had eaten today and would be able to eat tomorrow too. Sometimes food is not just food. It's security and hope. I have to wonder how much security and hope the people of Good Shepherd Church provided through our donation to Loaves & Fishes. And I have to wonder how much security and hope you will provide for someone in need when you *move on what you are moved by.*

Questions for Reflection and Discussion

Write responses and other thoughts in the space below each question. If you are discussing the book in a small group, prepare for the meeting by writing answers in advance.

1. What were the key problems in Nehemiah's community in Nehemiah 5? Who were the key players, and what did each party need to do in order to make things right?

2. Read Nehemiah 5:14-19. What example did Nehemiah set as governor of Judah? How did this message reinforce the reforms he attempted to make?

3. As you consider the circumstances in Jerusalem during Nehemiah's time, do you see any similar situations in our world today? What needs to happen to make these situations right?

4. Name a movie, documentary, story, or situation that has moved you. Why did it have such an impact on you? What emotions did it stir up? How did you respond?

5. The message noted the short distance between Nehemiah's emotion and his action. What is the distance between your emotions and your actions? What risk do we take when we act quickly? What risk do we take when we act too slowly?

6. How can we balance the need for careful thought with action as we respond to the needs we see in the world?

Move on What Moves You

This week, find what it is that moves you. Pay attention to your local community, and identify a need that raises your emotions. Then move on it: Take one concrete action to do something about it, trusting God to work through you to make the situation better. If you are reading this book in a study group, consider identifying the same need and coming up with a group response. What are you moved by, and how will you move on it?

Closing Prayer

God, thank you for the resources you have given us and for the privilege of sharing from those resources. Fill us knowledge; fill us with emotion; fill us with anger and sympathy. Fill us with your Holy Spirit and move us to action so that we can respond with generosity. In all of this, may your name be glorified. Amen.

Daily Scripture Readings

Monday: James 2:14-26
Tuesday: Matthew 25:31-46
Wednesday: Leviticus 19:1-10
Thursday: Proverbs 14:31; 28:27
Friday: Isaiah 58:1-13

OPPOSITIONISTS

"Don't be afraid of them! Remember that the Lord is great and awesome!" (Nehemiah 4:14b)

Everybody has a *Sanballat the Horonite*. Sanballat the Horonite is the name of Nehemiah's adversary, the "oppositionist" to Nehemiah's "solutionist." He's the guy who opposes Nehemiah's plans and activity at every turn, a thorn in Nehemiah's side who does everything he can to prevent the reconstruction of Jerusalem's wall and gates. And the presence of this staunch opposition isn't unique to Nehemiah. You and I also, somewhere in our lives, have a Sanballat the Horonite. We encounter adversity, and very often it comes in the form of another person who opposes our plans. The good news, though, is that we can draw insight from Nehemiah's response about how to react to our own oppositionists.

Remember what's going on in the Book of Nehemiah. It was around 445 B.C., and the people of Judah were exiled in 587 B.C. after the city of Jerusalem was destroyed. In 539 B.C. many of the people were allowed to return, meaning they had been back in Jerusalem for just over a hundred years. They'd rebuilt the Temple, but much of the rest of the city was still a wreck. According to the report Nehemiah received, the wall remained broken down, the gates remained burned, and the people were "in great trouble and shame" (Nehemiah 1:3). With the city wall still in shambles, the people lacked the security it could provide. Again, it was 445 B.C. So because Nehemiah was not one of those who points out problems but instead pinpoints solutions, he left his place of luxury in the Persian king's court, traveled hundreds of miles to Jerusalem, and began to galvanize the city's residents to rebuild the wall. Nehemiah was a solutionist with an uncanny knack for rallying co-solutionists around him, leading and inspiring them to accomplish more than they thought possible. As we saw in chapter 2, Nehemiah took inventory and opened their eyes to the damage they'd gotten used to. And as we discussed in the last chapter, Nehemiah took decisive action to remedy some of the social problems that were also plaguing the community.

All the while, however, Nehemiah had to deal with another dilemma: Not only did he battle impersonal obstacles and social ills; he also faced active opposition from a man named Sanballat the Horonite, who wanted to bring Jerusalem's reconstruction to a halt. It started before Nehemiah's reconstruction project even got underway, with Sanballat and another official becoming angry when they heard of Nehemiah's arrival in Jerusalem and support from the Persian king (Nehemiah 2:10). Most likely Sanballat was a government official of another nearby province. The Elephantine Papyri, which date to 407 B.C., identify Sanballat as the governor of Samaria, just to the north of Judah. Nehemiah's arrival, then, aroused rivalry and enmity from Samaria and its governor.[1] Sanballat immediately saw that Nehemiah was a threat to his position. In addition, like a lot of people, he actually seemed to like it when things were broken and in disarray. At least that's the impression we get from his heavy opposition.

Sanballat becomes angry as soon as Nehemiah arrives, but his opposition begins in earnest in chapter 4 while the wall reconstruction is in progress. Here is the reaction from Sanballat, Tobiah, and the other oppositionists, as well as Nehemiah's response to them:

> [1] When Sanballat heard that we were building the wall, he became angry and raged. He mocked the Jews, [2] saying in the presence of his associates and the army of Samaria: "What are those feeble Jews doing? Will they restore things themselves? Will they offer sacrifices? Will they finish it in a day? Will they revive the stones from the piles of rubble, even though they are burned?"
>
> [3] Tobiah the Ammonite, who was beside him, added: "If even a fox climbs on whatever they build, their wall of stones will crumble."
>
> [4] Listen, God; we are despised! Turn their insults to us back on their heads and make them like plunder in a captive land. [5] Don't forgive their iniquity or blot out their sins from your sight. They have thrown insults at the builders!
>
> [6] We continued to build the wall. All of it was joined together, and it reached half of its intended height because the people were eager to work. [7] But when Sanballat, Tobiah, the Arabs, the Ammonites, and the people of Ashdod heard that the work on the walls was progressing and the gaps were being closed, they were very angry. [8] They plotted together to come and fight against Jerusalem and to create a disturbance in it.
>
> [9] So we prayed to our God and set a guard as protection against them day and night.

¹⁰ But in Judah it was said,

> "The carrier's strength is failing,
>
> for there is too much rubble.
>
> We are unable to rebuild the wall!"

¹¹ Meanwhile, our enemies were saying: "Before they know or see anything, we can be in their midst and start to kill them. We'll stop the work!"

¹² Now the Jews who were living near them came and said to us again and again, "You must return to us!"

¹³ So I took up a position in the lowest parts of the space behind the wall in an open area. Then I stationed the people by families, and they had their swords, spears, and bows. ¹⁴ After reviewing this, I stood up and said to the officials, the officers, and the rest of the people, "Don't be afraid of them! Remember that the Lord is great and awesome! Fight for your families, your sons, your daughters, your wives, and your houses!"

¹⁵ Then our enemies heard that we had found out and that God had spoiled their plans. So we all returned to doing our own work on the wall. ¹⁶ But from that day on, only half of my workers continued in the construction, while the other half held the spears, shields, bows, and body armor. Meanwhile, the leaders positioned themselves behind the whole house of Judah, ¹⁷ who were building the wall. The carriers did their work with a load in one hand and a weapon in the other. ¹⁸ The builders built with swords fastened in their belts, and the trumpeter stayed by my side.

¹⁹ Then I said to the officials, the officers, and the rest of the people, "The work is very spread out, and we are far apart from each other along the wall. ²⁰ When you hear the trumpet sound, come and gather where we are. Our God

will fight for us!" [21] So we continued the work, with half of them holding spears from dawn until dusk.

[22] I also said to the people at that time, "Let every man and his servant spend the night in Jerusalem so that we can guard during the night and work during the day." [23] Neither I nor my relatives, nor my servants, nor my bodyguards took off our clothes, even when they sent for water.

We can almost imagine the ancient equivalent of beeping trucks, portable toilets as mandated by the state, and permit signs all over the place. The very rumor of such a site caused Sanballat to become angry and rage, mocking the Jews for their efforts to rebuild Jerusalem (Nehemiah 4:1-2). Anger at Nehemiah's arrival (2:10) became rage and mocking as construction began. Today we might call Sanballat a hater, someone who speaks ill of another person's plans and success. Except that Sanballat didn't stop at negative words. His opposition escalated even further when the wall was completed to half its height around the whole city. Sanballat and his associates became "very angry" and plotted to come and fight against the builders to prevent them from completing their work.

Nehemiah responded by preparing for an attack, encouraging the people of Jerusalem that God is with them (verses 13-14). His precautions worked, and Sanballat and the others didn't follow through with their plans. Nehemiah continued to be cautious, however, and he continued work on the wall, with the people prepared for another attack. He set guards, armed the builders, and kept trumpets at the ready to draw everyone into quick formation if necessary (verses 15-19). Such precautions slowed the work down, but they also did the job and prevented an attack.

Of course, that didn't stop Sanballat's opposition, however. We see it crop up again in chapter 6, with Sanballat and his fellow haters trying to set up an ambush for Nehemiah: "Now when Sanballat, Tobiah, Geshem the Arab, and the rest of our enemies heard that I had rebuilt the wall and that there were no gaps left in it (although I hadn't yet hung the doors in the gates), Sanballat and Geshem sent me this message: 'Come, let's meet together in one of the villages in the plain of Ono'" (Nehemiah 6:1-2).In other words, "Let's meet out here in the middle of nowhere—just to talk." Yeah, right. Fortunately, our solutionist Nehemiah didn't fall for the trap. Four times he told them that he was too busy with his important work of reconstruction and didn't have time to come for a meeting (Nehemiah 6:3-4). Even then Sanballat didn't stop, threatening to report that Nehemiah was rebelling against Persia (which was a lie) and hiring prophets to intimidate him (Nehemiah 6:6-7, 10-13). But Nehemiah was both cunning and persistent, and eventually he completed the wall with the help of God (Nehemiah 6:15-16).

At every turn, for every solution he devised, Nehemiah ran headlong into opposition. He came face to face with this hater, Sanballat the Horonite. For a busy man with lots to do and a wall to build, dealing with that resistance had to have been such a hassle, not to mention how dangerous it was.

EVERYBODY HAS A SANBALLAT THE HORONITE.

All of this opposition probably sounds familiar to you; as I said at the beginning of this chapter, everybody has a Sanballat the Horonite. It's all the more true for you if you pursue God's solutions, like Nehemiah did. We all have had someone in our life who represented resistance, hostility, opposition. We all have had—dare I say it—haters. Sometimes this opposition, this hate, comes even from the people who by all rights should love you the most, the people who should be on your side. As an example, a while back I recently heard of some Methodist colleagues of mine who take issue with the volume of water we use in baptism at Good Shepherd. We do full immersion, and they are apparently sprinklers; they would just as soon have me not in The United Methodist Church. One person even called me a "formerly Methodist pastor" online. In a previous church I served, someone wondered whether I should be a holiness pastor, since we were introducing some informality in worship and she preferred a more formal liturgy. (Ironically, holiness churches have their roots in Methodism.) So as a pastor, I've received opposition from fellow Christians, even fellow Methodists, for the kind of worship that I lead.

I had a Sanballat even earlier in my life, when I was a kid. On the tennis court, I had a nemesis who beat me fifteen times in a row. Most of those times, it made him the number one player in Texas for our age group and me number two. It was quite a rivalry; you can tell that it had quite the effect on me, because I still remember it forty years later. I have had seasons of my life where I've wanted to go somewhere or do something, and at every turn someone or something stood in opposition. And I've found that the more you seek God's solutions, the more opposition you can expect.

I know you've had Sanballats, too. It might be the guy at work. You have ideas; you work for progress; you value innovation; and you do what you can to bring about good, needed changes. But his priority is preservation and resistance, so he works against you to preserve the status quo and to stymie your efforts. In fact, you

THE MORE YOU SEEK GOD'S SOLUTIONS, THE MORE OPPOSITION YOU CAN EXPECT.

suspect sometimes that he likes everything at work that is broken and burnt. Even if it's not active opposition, it's the constant voice of a hater, telling you that your solution won't work, giving you the reasons you will fail. Actually, that type of resistance is nothing new. There's a story that's told about Robert Fulton, the man who built the first steamboat. When he first sailed it on the Hudson River, a skeptic was on the dock calling out, "It'll never start! It'll never start!" And then it did start. So the hater edited himself, and began calling out, "It'll never stop! It'll never stop!" I've got to think that someone will read that story and wonder how in the world the same guy has shown up at his workplace.

Maybe for you, the Sanballat is closer to home. Maybe it's not someone at work but one of your family members, maybe even your own mother or father. Or both. Some families just seem to have a knack for sabotaging and undermining. I have seen young people trying to get out of trouble and get into recovery, and the family doesn't even support that. Situations like that are truly some of the saddest I encounter in ministry. Sometimes hate and opposition come from the very ones who should provide love and support.

For others of you, maybe your Sanballat has to do with faith. Maybe you constantly encounter opposition to your own growth into a living relationship with Jesus Christ. Or maybe you want to advance ministry, try something new, reach more people, or serve in a different way; but you meet resistance. You meet the people who say, "We've never done it that way before." Or the people who say, "We did something like that a while back, so it's not worth trying again." Or worse, the people who say, "That's a great idea!" and then work against you behind the scenes. These things happen in church; opposition crops up everywhere. In church, out of church, at work, or at home, you have your Sanballats; and I have mine. And they are such hassles.

What do we do when we encounter opposition like this? Do we hope or pray for something like that great Irish toast? "May those that love us, love us. And those that don't love us, may God turn their hearts. And if he doesn't turn their hearts, may he turn their ankles so we'll know them by their limping." Should we pray something like that? Or should we pack up and go home, concluding that our efforts must not be God's will if the road is so tough? Or do we get ready to fight, putting on the gloves and going to the mat? What can we learn from Nehemiah about how to respond to our Sanballats, our haters, our oppositionists?

NEHEMIAH TURNS TO GOD.

If we look closely at Nehemiah's responses to Sanballat, we will discover a telling pattern. First consider Nehemiah's reply to Sanballat and the others in 2:20: "The God of heaven will give us success! ... As God's servants, we will start building. But you will have no share, right, or claim in Jerusalem." Next consider his words in 4:4-5, which he directs to God in prayer: "Listen, God; we are despised! Turn their insults to us back on their heads and make them like plunder in a captive land. Don't forgive their iniquity or blot out their sins from your sight. They have thrown insults at the builders!" Finally, read Nehemiah's account of the response to the wall's completion in 6:16: "When our enemies heard about this, all of the nations around us were afraid and their confidence was greatly shaken. They knew that this work was completed with the help of our God." In every instance, Nehemiah turns to God. He expresses confidence in God. He prays directly to God. And he attributes success to God. Opposition drives Nehemiah closer to God, and he recognizes God as the source of the wall's success time and time again.

This is an important point, because Nehemiah is a capable individual. He is supremely self-confident. He is accomplished. He is talented. He might even be a tad bit cocky. And like any capable, successful person, his tendency would have been to trust in himself and his considerable skills in managing projects and people. God must have known how dangerous that would be for Nehemiah and the people of Jerusalem. No doubt, Nehemiah could have gotten the wall built without divine assistance; but the result would have been Nehemiah's wall and not God's wall. God loves Nehemiah way too much to allow that to happen. And because Nehemiah faced opposition, he turned to God. And God was able to work through him.

In a way, the opposition that Nehemiah encountered was a gift. Those haters, those adversaries, those enemies were a gift. They were not a hassle, but an honor. Sanballat, Tobiah, and the others were for Nehemiah an on-going reminder that his work would really be fruitful only if he relied fully on God's help and strength. God allowed Nehemiah to tell him that he couldn't do

74

it so that he could discover that God *can* do it. The opposition made Nehemiah desperate; and in his desperation, he turned to God. By doing that, he opened himself to God working in him and through him. The opposition did not distract him from the work so much as it focused him on the Lord. Sanballat's hostility was a gift to Nehemiah because it allowed God's strength to show through. So from Nehemiah's response in the face of adversity, we can uncover a new attitude toward the opposition that we encounter: ***God gives opposition to grow desperation.***

Every Sanballat we face, every obstacle we encounter, can be viewed as a promise, not a problem. Each is a promise that God wants to accomplish in you and through you something bigger and better and deeper than what you could accomplish on your own. Your Sanballats are not your hassle; they are your honor. Instead of viewing them as a setback to lament, we can choose to view them as a gift to be received. *God gives opposition to grow desperation.*

GOD GIVES OPPOSITION TO GROW DESPERATION.

Who is your Sanballat? Who is your opposition in your family, at your work, regarding your faith, or even in your church? What if you were to thank God for that person, recognizing that he or she is driving you away from self-reliance and toward dependence on God? Paul writes that when he is weak, then he is strong (2 Corinthians 12:10). We find strength in weakness, success in failure, because only when our own strength fails do we turn to God to find true, divine power. What you think is pitiful, God regards as beautiful. It looks to you like failure; God regards it as faith. *God gives opposition to grow desperation.*

My prayer for each of us is that we might stop looking at our Sanballats as hassles and start regarding them as promises from God. My prayer is that we might see insurmountable challenges or relentless opposition as opportunities for God's power to show up in our lives.

Let me conclude with a couple of practical tips we can also glean from Nehemiah when it comes to our oppositionists.

DON'T DEFEND YOURSELF. MANY SANBALLATS OPERATE BY DISTRACTION.

First: Don't defend yourself. Many, many Sanballats operate by distraction. Their goal is to distract you from what you need to be doing. They seek to control a situation by asking questions that don't need to be answered. That's worth repeating: Some people seek to control a situation by asking questions that don't need to be answered. That's what Sanballat and Tobiah did. They asked

Nehemiah and the builders, "What are you doing? ... Are you rebelling against the king?" (Nehemiah 2:19). They even turned this question into a formal accusation with which they threatened Nehemiah (see Nehemiah 6:6-7). All of this amounted to a distraction that didn't deserve a reply. Nehemiah had official royal backing from the beginning of his journey; he didn't need to bother answering their question or their accusation. Nehemiah wisely recognized their question for what it was: a distraction. And he didn't let it side-track him.

You can waste all kinds of time and all kinds of energy trying to answer what can't be, and shouldn't be, answered at all. I remember back at Christmas in 2010, when Good Shepherd Church did the sermon series called *What Child Is This?* The congregation gave $207,000 to fight sex trafficking in India. It was incredible, and girls are walking free today because of the good work we did that Christmas. I got a note not long after Christmas Eve that year, which asked the question: "Where was the star?" We hadn't gone all-out on Christmas stage décor that year because we had a higher calling to free girls being raped for profit. But where was the star? I have to tell you, if your takeaway from a Christmas Eve about freedom for sex slaves was that your decorated Bethlehem star got taken away, who has time to address that? I didn't. Don't defend yourself. Depend on God.

Second: Keep at it. I said earlier that Sanballats love to turn your attention and your energy away from the important work you are called to do. If they can't stop the work, they will try to slow it down. Sanballat and the others tried to lure Nehemiah into an ambush, sending messengers five different times to call him to a meeting (Nehemiah 6:1-7). His response each time is simple: "I'm doing important work, so I can't come down. Why should the work stop while I leave it to come down to you?" I love that. Nothing fancy, just "I'm busy!" And so are you. After you thank God for that oppositionist reminder to lean on God more, put your head down and get back to work. Nehemiah's relentless focus on the work of the wall—which was really God's work—allowed him to push through, despite the heavy opposition that he faced. That kind of focus is a good example for us to follow. In 2011, almost everything about Good Shepherd Church changed. Why? Because, as I mentioned in Chapter 2, we refocused ourselves singularly around our mission of inviting all people into a living relationship with Jesus Christ. The power and focus of that mission puts the words of Nehemiah 6:3 in all of our mouths: I'm doing important work, so I can't come down." I get up every day, wondering, "What massively small step can this church take today to invite all people into a living relationship with Jesus Christ?"

We can learn a lot from Nehemiah's response to his enemies. But the most important insight is this: Opposition isn't the enemy. Self-reliance is. It's about God, not us. And Nehemiah's enemies were a gift, precisely because they moved him to recognize that crucial fact. Every time he encountered their hostility, he turned to God. Look again at the irony of Nehemiah 6:16: "All of the nations around us were afraid and their confidence was greatly shaken. They knew that this work was completed with the help of our God." Nehemiah was not afraid of his oppositionists; they were afraid of his God. When we are weak, then we are strong. *God gives opposition to grow desperation.*

Questions for Reflection and Discussion

Write responses and other thoughts in the space below each question. If you are discussing the book in a small group, prepare for the meeting by writing answers in advance.

1. Look closely at Nehemiah chapters 2, 4, and 6. What forms does Sanballat's opposition take? What makes him so relentless in his hostility toward Nehemiah and the Jerusalem wall?

2. Note the practical steps that Nehemiah takes in response to Sanballat's threats in Nehemiah 4. How did these specific actions work with, or against, Nehemiah's spirit of reliance upon God?

3. How can you blend practical action with dependence upon God in your own life?

4. What characterizes modern-day Sanballats? Think of examples from your own life. How did you respond to them?

5. Have you ever acted as a Sanballat toward someone else? What motivated your opposition?

6. The message above claims that what we find pitiful, God regards as beautiful. What does this mean? Have you ever seen failure turn into faith? What was the situation, and what was the result of it?

7. This chapter challenges us to have an attitude of thankfulness toward opposition. How does this encourage you or inspire you?

Thank God for Opposition

This week, give thanks to God for the opposition you face, whether in the form of other people or of impersonal obstacles that you encounter. Recognize in them an opportunity to rely on God more fully than you have before.

Closing Prayer

Father in heaven, we come before you today with an odd gratitude. We thank you today for our problems. We thank you for those who disagree with us, for those who don't like us, for those who have wronged us, and for those who ignore us. We thank you even for those who, like Sanballat, have opposed all of our good ideas. We praise you, Lord, for those problems that show us our need to rely on you more than upon ourselves. We yield ourselves more fully to you today, asking that all of our human opposition might grow godly desperation in us. Amen.

Daily Scripture Readings

Monday: 2 Corinthians 1:1–2:4
Tuesday: 2 Corinthians 2:5–3:6
Wednesday: 2 Corinthians 3:7–4:18
Thursday: 2 Corinthians 7:2-16; 10:1-18
Friday: 2 Corinthians 12:1-21

1. From *The CEB Study Bible With Apocrypha,* edited by Joel B. Green et al. (Common English Bible, 2013); page 741 OT.

5

THE BEAUTY OF NAME DROPPING

Then Eliashib the high priest set to work with his fellow priests and built the Sheep Gate…. The people of Jericho built next to them. (Nehemiah 3:1a, 2a)

Many people leave their marks on the world, don't they? They live in such a way that when they're gone, something of their presence on earth remains. For instance, I'd say the Wright Brothers left their mark. In my home state of North Carolina, their legacy adorns every license plate with the proud tag line: *"First in Flight."* More significantly, every plane flight today owes something to their pioneering work. Likewise, Ben Franklin left his mark; and his likeness can be found on the front of every $100 bill. We even call them "Benjamins." Steve Jobs left his mark as well, as anyone with an iPad, iPhone, or even one of those old antique iPods can attest.

Leaving a mark on the world can be negative as well. Every time you go through airport security you know, sadly, that Osama Bin Laden has left his mark on planet earth. In even more recent days, many people note with approval the practice of law enforcement to avoid naming mass murderers publicly—a practice that denies mass murderers the very infamy they long for. Despite this practice, though, shooters from Columbine to Sandy Hook have left their wicked marks on the world. In ways large and small, famous and infamous, from movements to monuments, for good and ill, folks all around the word have left their mark.

And probably some of you readers want to leave a mark, as well. Most of you probably don't really want to have to *die* to do it; you would just as soon leave a mark at your school, on your team, or at your job and then move on to the next accomplishment. But since all of us will die sooner or later, at some point you'll have to consider the kind of ultimate mark you'll leave on the world. This is especially true when you get to be a certain age and know that you have less time in front of you than you have behind you. And yet, it's also true when you're young and getting started and have some ambition. You want to leave the world with some indication that you were here. Most of us, I think it's safe to assume, want to leave a *positive* mark on the world—one like Steve Jobs left, rather than a wretched one like Osama Bin Laden left behind. Most of us think of leaving a mark in terms of accomplishments: Our mark will be one thing, or perhaps a collection of things, that we have done. But actually, as we dig down into this final chapter of *Solve*, we will see that it's something much, much different. Much better. More attainable. Leaving our mark is less about *what* and more about *who*.

I say all that because of Nehemiah, our favorite solution seeker. To this point, we have seen his remarkable determination. We've studied his deft way of dealing with adversaries, and we've been moved by his ability to mobilize people to pinpoint solutions to a city-wide famine. We've seen him humbly confess his people's sins and turn to God's promises. And through it all, we've been wooed by his contagious brand of optimism. But I want to conclude our study with an unexpected insight, which we uncover in an oddly placed section of Nehemiah's memoir, Nehemiah chapter 3. Why do I say that this chapter is oddly placed? Because the material in chapter 3 seems to assume that the Jerusalem wall, the driving force in the whole Book of Nehemiah, has been completed. But in the larger Nehemiah narrative, which continues in Nehemiah 4, the mighty Jerusalem wall's construction is still underway. It's as if someone has taken the epilogue at the end of the story and moved it to the middle. It interrupts the story's tension with an interlude that does nothing to advance the plot.

NAMES, TASKS, AND CONTINUITY

Moreover, as we prepare to enter the unique territory of Nehemiah 3, I want to alert you ahead of time: What you're going to read contains no riveting drama. No high-stakes conflict. No whodunit. Not even any clever wordplay or insightful turns of phrase. Instead, what Nehemiah includes in this section is a rather long list. It's a list of who did the work on which part of the Jerusalem wall. This material is boring and seems out of place, but I think that the author has included it here to tell us something important about what Nehemiah values and deems worthy of recording. It gives us Nehemiah's subtle clues about what is involved in leaving your mark on the world. Nehemiah 3 might be tedious reading, but embedded within that tedium are some important theological insights and personal brilliance that we simply can't afford to miss.

Look first at 3:1-2:

> [1] Then Eliashib the high priest set to work with his fellow priests and built the Sheep Gate. They dedicated it and set up its doors, then dedicated it as far as the Tower of the Hundred and as far as the Tower of Hananel.
> [2] The people of Jericho built next to them, and Zaccur, Imri's son, built next to them.

The chapter begins with a list of names and tasks, emphasizing continuity between them. Names: Eliashib, Zaccur, Imri. Tasks: building the Sheep Gate and setting up its doors. Continuity: Men of Jericho build an adjoining section "next to them," and Zaccur builds "next to them." Names, tasks, and continuity. Note that pattern, because we will see it again. And again. And again.

For example, here are the next verses, Nehemiah 3:3-5:

> [3] The children of Hassenaah built the Fish Gate; they laid its beams and set up its doors, bolts, and bars. [4] Next to them Meremoth, Uriah's son and Hakkoz's grandson, made repairs. Meshullam, Berechiah's son and Meshezabel's grandson, made repairs next to them, and Zadok, Baana's son, made repairs next to them. [5] Next to them the people from Tekoa made repairs, but their officials wouldn't help with the work of their supervisors.

More names: the children of Hassenaah, Meremoth, Meshullam, Zadok, and the people from of Tekoa. More tasks: beams, doors, bolts, and bars. And more continuity: "made repairs next to them." And then a delicious bit of gossip: The Tekoan nobles refuse to get their hands dirty. This brings to mind a marvelous law of leadership: People won't follow where they don't see you going.

The pattern continues (3:6-12):

> ⁶Joiada, Paseah's son, and Meshullam, Besodeiah's son, repaired the Mishneh Gate; they laid its beams and set up its doors, bolts, and bars. ⁷Next to them repairs were made by Melatiah the Gibeonite, Jadon the Meronothite, and the people of Gibeon and of Mizpah, who were ruled by the governor of the province Beyond the River.
>
> ⁸Uzziel, Harhaiah's son, one of the goldsmiths, made repairs next to them; and Hananiah, one of the perfumers, made repairs next to him. They restored Jerusalem as far as the Broad Wall. ⁹Next to them Rephaiah, Hur's son, ruler of half the district of Jerusalem, made repairs. ¹⁰Next to them Jedaiah, Harumaph's son, made repairs opposite his house, and Hattush, Hashabneiah's son, made repairs next to him.
>
> ¹¹Malchijah, Harim's son, and Hasshub, Pahath-moab's son, repaired another section and the Tower of the Ovens. ¹²Next to them Shallum, Hallohesh's son, ruler of half the district of Jerusalem, made repairs, along with his daughters.

Once again, we find more names, more tasks, and more continuity. And the primary repeated word is "next." It's one of those rich details that Nehemiah includes by design, showing us that the work continues side-by-side, with no interruptions. And in a variation from the usual form, this section even includes a bit of gender equality: Shallum repairs the next section "along with his daughters" (verse 12). Nehemiah, unfortunately, fails to mention their names. In this, he follows the conventions of his day. The men are named; the women are not. With my twenty-first century sensibilities, I want to shake my hero Nehemiah and say: "Tell their names too!" But that's asking Nehemiah to be a twenty-first century United Methodist rather than a fifth-century B.C. Jew. Sigh.

Finally, look at 3:13-14:

> [13] Hanun and the people of Zanoah repaired the Valley Gate; they built it and set up its doors, bolts, and bars. They also repaired fifteen hundred feet of the wall, as far as the Dung Gate.
>
> [14] Malchiah, Rechab's son, ruler of the district of Beth-haccherem, repaired the Dung Gate. He rebuilt it and set up its doors, bolts, and bars.

We find more names, more tasks, and more continuity in these verses too. We even see what is from modern perspective a bit of hilarity: the Dung Gate. What do you think that name did to the property values in its proximity? I suspect that it was not one of those zip codes in which all of the real estate agents wanted to work.

I will spare you further details of Nehemiah's list, but it goes on in the same vein through Nehemiah 3:32. It wraps its way around the circumference of Jerusalem, ending where it began, at the Sheep Gate. Frankly, this whole section of Nehemiah amounts to some heavy-duty name dropping. It's tedious, to be honest. It contains names we don't know, which are nearly impossible to pronounce. Most modern readers skim right over these names in order to get back to Nehemiah and the force of his personality as quickly as we can. Yet if we rush past this list, tedious as it is, we do so to our own detriment. Nehemiah includes this list for a reason, after all; we should pay attention to it.

For the purposes of *Solve,* I am slightly less interested in the list itself and rather more interested in Nehemiah's motives

NEHEMIAH CEASES TO BE A MEMOIR AND BECOMES A TRIBUTE.

for including it. Remember what genre the Book of Nehemiah represents: memoir. Now, a memoir is usually about me, all me, all the time. A memoir focuses on my thoughts, my feelings, my experiences, my reactions. A memoir is where you might encounter the sentiment "Enough about me, let's talk about you now. So tell me, what do you think about me?" But in this section of Nehemiah's memoir, whose name is conspicuously absent? The memoirist! No attention at all is given to Nehemiah himself; it's all about the others who contributed to the work on Jerusalem. That's why this section is not mere tedious name dropping. Instead, it opens a window into what Nehemiah finds important. This, in turn, shows us how we can authentically make our mark. In Nehemiah 3, the text ceases to be a memoir and becomes a tribute. It's a tribute to Eliashib, Joiada, Uzziel, the unnamed daughters of Shallum, and all the rest. Nehemiah skillfully deflects the attention from himself as leader and directs it onto those who did the work.

There's more. Not only is Nehemiah nowhere to be found in chapter 3, but the wall itself is largely absent as well. We do get a little bit of information about the major sections of the wall and the individuals and families who completed their construction. But think of all that Nehemiah left out in his description of the work. There are no descriptions of the scaffolding, the stones, the mortar, the masonry, the artisanship, the beasts of burden, or the tools needed to complete the project. The wall fades into the background as the names assume center stage. Otherwise-nameless folks receive

> LEAVING YOUR MARK ISN'T ABOUT WHAT YOU ACCOMPLISH. IT'S ABOUT WHO YOU INFLUENCE.

dignity and recognition by virtue of their mention in Nehemiah's list. These people get to see their names in lights.

When I add all the pieces together—Nehemiah's absence, the wall's disappearance, the seemingly endless list of names—it becomes clear what Nehemiah is doing. He is declaring to all who pay attention that this is the mark he's leaving on planet earth. This is his legacy. It's not the wall; it's the people he has motivated and galvanized and catalyzed to work on it. They are his enduring mark on the world. The people they became under his watch is his leadership gift to God. His legacy is not a wall; it's a people. He is less concerned with what he has built and more interested in the people he has built up. He may have been the licensed general contractor on the wall, but his real project was the community of people surrounding him. His mark is not a collection of "what;" it is an assemblage of "who."

This is where that subtle shift and thrilling realization leave us. This is what it means when a memoir transforms into a tribute: *Leaving your mark isn't about what you accomplish. It's about who you influence.*

Is there any message more urgent than this in a selfie world? Here is a man who measures success not when he sees his own name in lights, but when he sees the names of *others* in lights. That's Nehemiah's mark. And it's a pattern that we see in the New Testament as well. Jesus had the disciples whom he commissioned to carry on proclaiming the kingdom of God and baptizing in his name. Paul tells the Thessalonians that *they* are his joy and crown (1 Thessalonians 2:19). Paul has his Timothy, and Peter has his "son" Mark. The pattern established by Nehemiah and buttressed by the New Testament continues to this day. In a world that will seduce you into measuring your mark by *what*—the height of your skyscrapers, the size of your bank account, the number of your trophies—biblical faith goes back to *who*. *Leaving your mark isn't about what you accomplish. It's about who you influence.*

When the church gets it right, we help you find relational connections where that kind of influence can take place. It's why I particularly loved it when a young woman I know came into a meeting, and before we could even start, she just *had* to tell us about the small group she is part of. She said, "I feel like I am at a table of wisdom." When I pressed her on what that meant, she told me that she's the youngest in that group by ten years. These women were leaving their mark on her, and she recognized the value in it. She understood that they have lived long, loved well, and know Jesus; and she is at their feet soaking it up. Because these women have influenced her, she is "next" to the generation that has preceded her. She, along with our church community and those of you studying this together in a group, realizes that in circles and at tables is where life gets stronger. Her life is part of the mark these other women are leaving on the world.

BEFORE YOU CAN INFLUENCE OTHERS WELL, YOU FIRST NEED SOMEONE TO INFLUENCE YOU.

When we are able to leave a positive mark on others, it is because others have left such a mark on us. Be sure of this: before you can influence others well, you first need someone to influence you positively. Before you jump in and influence the next generation, make sure that you open yourself to the influence of a previous generation. My life has been thoroughly shaped by influencers, some of whom didn't even know I was paying such close attention. And in a real sense, my life is part of the mark those folks are leaving on earth.

I well remember that tennis coach I had when I was seventeen years old, Danny O'Bryant. One day, he gave me a remarkably simple piece of advice: Bend your knees on your backhand. Get your knees real low, finish with your racket real high, and watch what happens. What happened was that my backhand became a weapon, and nine months later—after a slew of runner-up finishes—I was holding the trophy as the Texas state champion. I am part of the mark Danny O'Bryant is leaving. *Leaving your mark isn't about what you accomplish. It's about who you influence.*

Ten years later, while studying for ministry, I served an internship at a church in Georgetown, Kentucky. The pastor, Elgan Reynolds, graciously allowed me to preach once a month. And yet for the first five or six times, he withheld any praise at all for my sermons. (I don't know if he knew it or not, but my love language is "words of affirmation"; and I wasn't getting any.) So before that next sermon, I resolved, "I'm going to do this one without any notes. Maybe then he'll tell me I'm doing a good job." So I did it. When I was finished, he leaned over and whispered, "You're gonna be OK." Affirmation received. And I haven't used notes since that time. Today's sermons at Good Shepherd are part of Elgan Reynold's mark on the world. *Leaving your mark isn't about what you accomplish. It's about who you influence.*

Later, as a young pastor in Monroe, North Carolina, I watched with awe and wonder as a neighboring pastor, Lenny Stadler, grew Weddington United Methodist Church. Under his leadership, the church reached the then-uncharted territory of more than one thousand people in worship each Sunday. He did it with an evangelistic fervor and revivalistic stamp that made him completely unique among United Methodist pastors. He showed me what was possible in ministry when you simplify the proclamation and multiply its impact. In a real sense, the ministry of Good Shepherd is possible in 2016 because of the trail Lenny Stadler blazed in the 1990s. He died from colo-rectal cancer in 2012, but I as a pastor and this church I serve are part of the mark he has left on planet Earth. His mark is not a building he built, but a people he inspired. *Leaving your mark isn't about what you accomplish. It's about who you influence.* And to be an influencer, allow yourself to first be influenced.

But it doesn't stop there. Leaving your mark is more about *who* than *what*, right? You know what is at stake for a whole lot of people? Untapped potential. My great fear is that too many of us have become spiritual hoarders: those who come and receive Sunday after Sunday (OK, maybe every other Sunday). We sing songs, listen to powerful preaching, read edifying books; but all it amounts to is collecting spiritual stuff, because we never give any of it away. We never step out and give to those who are needy, allowing the good news of Jesus Christ to make us more generous.

We never tell someone else about our faith, keeping that good news for ourselves. We don't invest in the next generation or in our fellow members of this generation. If that is the case, then we are missing out on a huge opportunity to influence others, a huge opportunity to leave our mark on the world by sharing Christ's love.

HOW ABOUT WE REPENT OF SPIRITUAL HOARDING?

Well, God help me if I ever get content with that, if I'm ever satisfied just because a good number of people come to hear our musicians sing and hear me yak! I know for sure that there is so much untapped potential at Good Shepherd Church. I am convinced that if people would stop hoarding blessings and experiences and failures and wisdom and would start giving that away in ministry, the marks we'd leave in terms of the lives we touch would be simply incredible. You—yes, *you*!—have the gifts, the wisdom, the experience, the traumas, and the favor that the next generation needs to receive. Instead of hoarding all that God has done in our lives, how about we pour it out? Usually when we talk about repenting, we speak of it in terms of sin. How about we reorient that today? How about we repent of hoarding? Repent of lack of involvement, lack of influence? Instead of "go and sin no more," it's "go and get involved." Like Nehemiah, recognize that true greatness happens not when your name is in lights but when someone you have influenced receives the light of Christ. *Leaving your mark isn't about what you accomplish. It's about who you influence.*

In the way children's and student ministries work at our church, we're always looking for one more voice to augment what parents are already saying. That partnership is what kids need. When you combine the light of the church with the love of the home, you form a child to have a living relationship with Jesus Christ from the youngest of ages. And that's why we are always looking for adults who will be that *one more voice* in the life of a child in our church. Relationships are so much more important than programming for us. In fact, the only purpose of programming is to set up the possibility of relationships. What difference would it make at your church if programming were not an end in and of itself but merely a platform to set up the possibility of relationships? What would it look like in your own life if you were to allow God to take all of your experiences, your successes, your failures, your archived knowledge—even the wisdom you're gaining from this study— and then shared it with someone in an emerging generation? Nehemiah's people were building a wall side-by-side, "next to" one another. In the twenty-first-century church, we need folks who stand next to the generation that comes after them. *Leaving your mark isn't about what you accomplish. It's about who you influence.*

Mike Breen, who leads a ministry called 3D Movements, speaks helpfully about the difference in church world between delivering services and developing people. All too often, churches have focused on delivering Sunday morning services: providing captivating music, compelling messages, and stirring videos. Breen suggests a reorientation in which we move our ministries from the delivery model to the development model. In other words, we must develop people who have been deeply influenced so that they can, in turn, become deep influencers.

That's not the easiest shift of a mindset for me. Good Shepherd has long been in delivery mode, attempting through each sermon series to outdo the one that came before it. And yet, shortly before I heard from Mike Breen, a trusted advisor told me to embrace the fact that I am now over fifty years old (!) and have a limited number of years left to share some of my pastoral strength, hope, and knowledge with the next generation of church leaders. So I am making some early attempts to live into that "second half" kind of calling, praying that my mark on this world will be in young clergy with names such as Andrea and Matt and Daniel and Devin. My mark—our mark—will not be in any building that Good Shepherd builds, but in people we build up.

Because maybe, just maybe, I'll be like Nehemiah: When it's time for me to write a memoir, by God's grace, it will become a tribute instead. How about you? What mark will you leave on the world? *Leaving your mark isn't about what you accomplish. It's about who you influence.*

Questions for Reflection and Discussion

Write responses and other thoughts in the space below each question. If you are discussing the book in a small group, prepare for the meeting by writing answers in advance.

1. How do you usually respond when you encounter lists (genealogies, land allotments, or similar things) in Scripture? Based on the reflection above, why might such lists be important?

2. The individuals and groups named in Nehemiah 3 were each responsible for one section of the Jerusalem wall. What does this tell us about the work and the way they went about it? What lessons can we draw from this passage about work in the church and in the world today?

3. How does Nehemiah's model of leadership inspire you? How does it challenge you?

THE BEAUTY OF NAME DROPPING

4. Who have been the key people who have influenced you?
    Who have "left a mark" on you?

5. Whom have you influenced? If leaving your mark is
    more about people you influence rather than your
    accomplishments, how would you characterize the mark
    you have left on the world thus far?

6. What opportunities do you see around you to leave your mark on the world by influencing people with the good news of Jesus Christ?

Leave a Mark

This week, focus on your relationships with other people. Recognize and celebrate the positive influence that others have had on you, and notice also the ways in which you influence the people around you. What can you do to invest more time and energy into the people you are influencing? How can you focus less on accomplishments and more on these people?

Closing Prayer

Dear God, we thank you for all of the people you have put into our lives to influence us toward you. Please help us see the opportunities all around us to influence others so that we might leave a good mark on the world. In Jesus' name, we pray. Amen.

Daily Scripture Readings

Monday: Nehemiah 3:1-21
Tuesday: Nehemiah 3:22-32
Wednesday: 1 Timothy 4:1-16
Thursday: 2 Timothy 1:1-7
Friday: 2 Timothy 3:10–4:22

Other Studies
by Talbot Davis

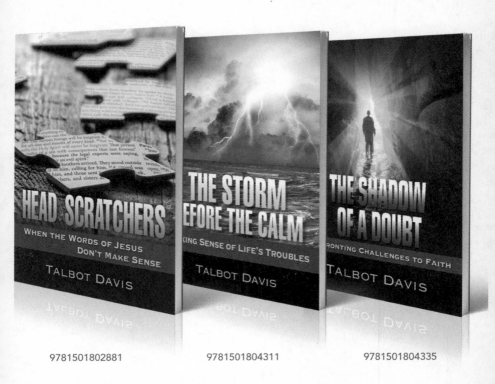

9781501802881   9781501804311   9781501804335

Order your copies today and continue studying with Davis.

Adult ministry resources, **together at last.**

Meet your newest companion, your brand-new assistant, and an innovative extension of your ministry!

Sunday school curriculum, small-group studies, Bibles, supplies, forums, and more.

We'll take care of the details, so you can focus on what you do best.

AdultBibleStudies.com
Visit today!

BKM1566010AR016

Abingdon Press™
Growing in Life, Serving in Faith

JESUS TAUGHT WITH WORDS.
PAUL TAUGHT WITH PICTURES.

Introducing *The Parables of Paul: The Master of the Metaphor*

"The metaphor is a strange literary critter. It makes things clear by giving us a picture. It compels us to enter unexplored territory—and often without our realizing what it's doing."

For over 2,000 years, the church has looked to the apostle Paul and his letters in order to understand and follow the Christian life. Paul had his own compelling way of sharing Jesus' message with others, through the use of the metaphor—a brief, imaginative word picture that shows the same truth as a longer story.

From casting himself in the role of a slave, to presenting the Christian as a solider or an actor, or even showing how we are vessels in the King's house, Paul's gallery of enriching, life-changing story pictures paints for us an indelible picture of the Christian faith. A discussion guide is included for small group use.

Published by

Cokesbury.com | 800.672.1789
Community Resource Consultants